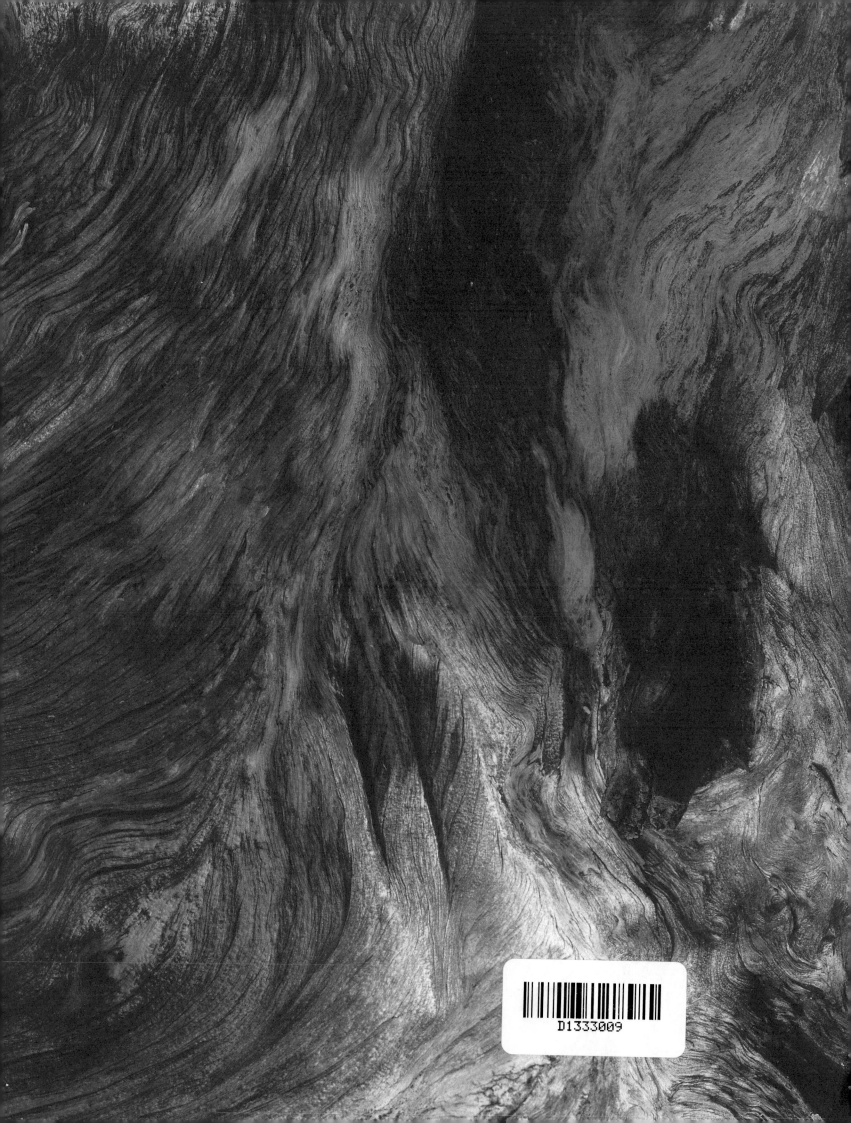

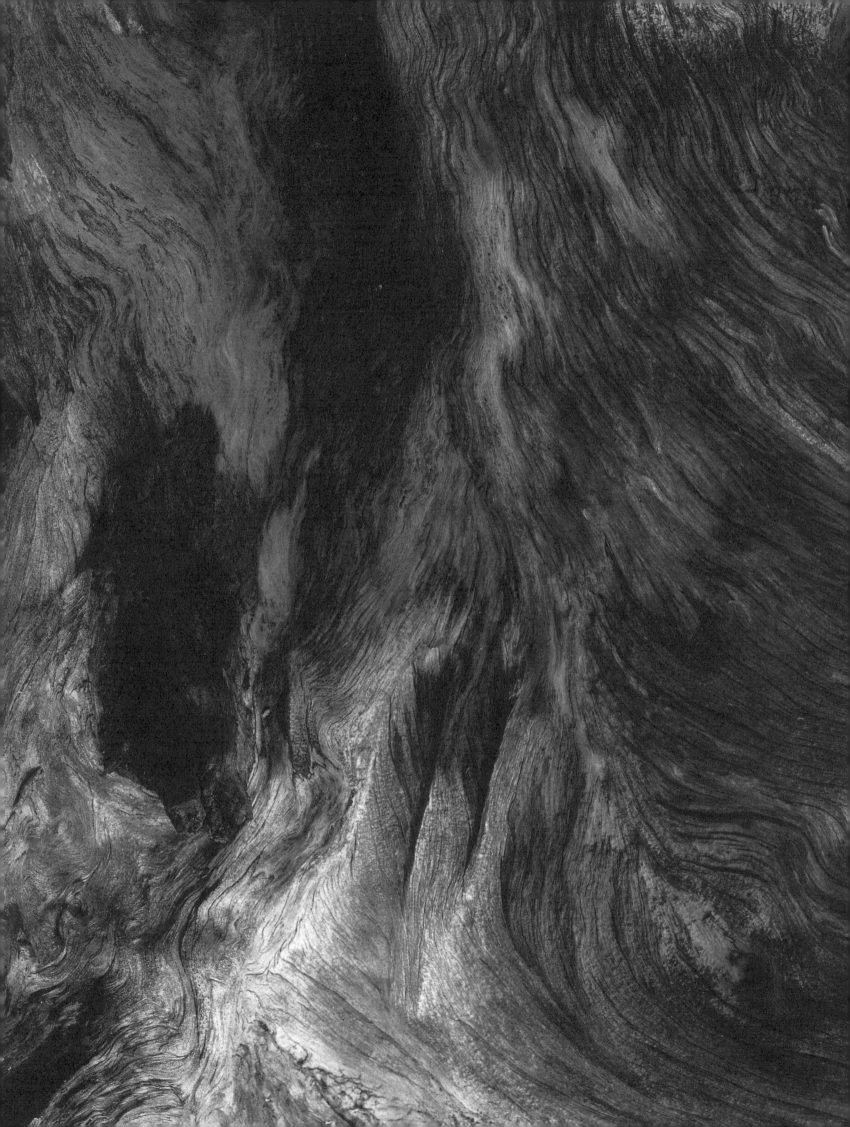

PANORAMA
NORWAY

The midnight sun sounds like a northern trumpet between the peaks of Flakstadøy, Lofoten.

A cornucopia of surprises....

Is Norway the realm of fjords? Definitely. Is Norway the realm of mountains? Oh yes. Is Norway a forest realm, a realm of lakes, an ocean realm? Of course. Norway is even the realm of Man. Not to mention the realm of the Northern Lights, the dark winters and the Midnight Sun - and the home of moose, salmon and men. And we must not forget that Norway is also the kingdom of the trolls and the spirits, the Nøkken water-sprite and the Huldra wood-nymph!!

Norway is a real cornucopia, a treasure-house of variety. It is the land that stands with her feet in the bad breath of the Central European ant-heap and stretches far enough to grip the edge of the Arctic ice with her fingertips. Mother Norway's lanky corpus has a variety and a multiplicity rivalled by few others. Here is landscape in every shape and form, and conditions that swing from the semi-Continental to the Arctic.

The hardiness of the country's inhabitants is equally impressive. Cod and the fisherman, reindeer and the Sami, sheep and the farmer, sparrow and the urbanite - all of them cheerfully defy blizzards, rain and cold to live here. But this is because they also enjoy such rich rewards: midnight sun and sparkling auroras, birdsong and multi-coloured flowering meadows, ski-tracks between snowy fir branches, roaring water-falls and sheltered bays for swimming. Norway is far from being an old crone sitting by the fire with a bent back - Mother Norway is in excellent shape, with roses in her cheeks and a spring in her step!

Now, nobody is trying to fool the reader that Norway is all pink skies and vio-lins. Norwegians are in general no smarter than other people, and they have scratched and tarnished their lovely country. Rivers are crammed into pipes, there is almost no virgin forest left and industry poisons the air and the water. Since there are, fortunately, not very many Norwegians in Norway, they have despite their best efforts not yet done their landscape as much damage as other peoples have inflicted on theirs. Moreover, there is reason to hope that the time will soon be ripe for economists to realise that the best long-term business for Norway is to be a green lung in an ever more urbanised world.

The country is large and the population is small, which means that you can still find places which are just as God left them. Moreover, you can go more or less where you will, access to the open country is protected by law. All the sensible inhabitants of the country make full use of this right, no one wears down more Vibram on stones and scree, no one scrapes their plastic skis more on crusted snow, than the average Norwegian.

To describe Norway in a new way is no easy task, many attempts have been made before. Facing this challenge I had the following idea: since Norway is such a long country, it must be described in long pictures! Only in this way will there be space for the variety and the lines, the power and the beauty that lie hidden in every panorama. This gives us a journey in time and space through the home of the Norwegians, with a new perspective, new insight!

We peep through all the doors, into all the rooms, under the blue or slate-grey roof. Many places we will greet with a nod of recognition: yes, between the cheery white wooden houses of the south coast, among the blazing autumn birches between fjord and snow, here we have been before. Looked at the hills beyond the hills beyond the hills, and the lunar landscape of the high plateaux. But wait, this we haven't seen before: the misty forest groped by the fingers of the sun, the blue light of the summer night, the pounding of the waves, the contorted rock of the mountain skyline. Can it be that the door to the other world was ajar when these pictures were taken, can it be that the film recorded something that your nine-to-five eyes failed to discern?

In this way a book like this can, I hope, tell a story that is rather different from the reality you yourself experience on your travels, whether you were born here with skis on your feet and knitted cap pulled over your eyes or are setting foot on Norwegian soil for the very first time. If you want to make your first voyage of discovery in this remarkable, sparsely populated land while standing on your dignity and with your nose in the air, well, you can expect that it will take you a while to get to know the soul of the country. But once you are bitten by the Norway bug, you will hardly want to go anywhere else in the four corners of the earth. For the Norwegian diamond has been cut with so many facets that you will never see the same one twice, however much you turn it. Even if you come back to exactly the same place, it is a different experience. The seasons, the weather, the light, the animals, the birds, plants and people - the blend is the never the same.

If you want to travel in Norway and start off on the right foot, just keep browsing in this book. But remember: warm clothes! Here you will meet both the cosy and the austere aspects of the country.

PÅL HERMANSEN

THE REALM OF THE FJORDS

The story of the fjord country is the story of an ocean
that met Norway and fell in love.
It was not content to throw its waves unrequited against the hard cliffs,
and refused to accept its rejection by such a beautiful land.
Who can blame it? And so what had to happen, happened.
The curious ocean went exploring and left long, winding silver trails behind it.
For the ocean saw that the land was so lovely that it lost all interest
in returning to where it really belonged.
And this is why there are still bright threads of salt sea deep
in the mountain kingdom, like an octopus with many long arms feeling
for Mother Norway's heart - not to do it any harm, of course,
but just to come close to it, feel her warmth and her pulse,
and perhaps also to do its beloved a service and ease the way for those
of her people who wanted to see the wide world.

*T*he ocean was in no hurry, it had several hundred million years before it. The land was pounded and kneaded by gigantic forces, huge masses collided, colossal mountains were pushed on top of one another. The land rose, and then it was once more kneaded and scraped by glaciers and roaring waters. And not just the once, but again and again. The last and decisive battle was fought in the Tertiary, 70-72 million years ago, when the land tipped so that the western rim rose in the air. In their desperation to reach the sea, wild waters threw themselves over the steep cliffs. They kept this up for millions of years and slowly but surely their channels ate themselves backwards into the mountain massifs, which came more and more to resemble an old, chipped sawhorse.

Then the climate changed, and the herds of elephant and hippopotamus in the coastal forests had to find somewhere else to live. The ice lay on the country like a sugared breastplate and greaves, and pressed deeper into the earth. Ten, fifteen or even twenty times the ice came and went. The saw-cuts made by the rivers gave the ice an extra good finger-grip, and the glaciers hunkered down in the channels and squirmed from side to side. The west-running valleys were thus widened and deepened, and the great gouges neared the ocean. When the ice gave up for the last time - so far - about 10,000 years ago, there was only a kind of doorstep left, a doorstep the ocean had no trouble stepping over. The friendly invasion was a fact.

The ancient mountains have watched the whole drama. They have watched the sun light flaming bonfires on the peaks when night gives way to day, and marvelled at the sculpting of the landscape and experienced the dramatic moment when the ocean flooded into the land and spread its glittering mirror between the bare cliffs.

The mountains rejoiced to see how the cold and barren land slowly became milder and softer, and started to dimple with woodlands and smile with grass and heather. Silver-trunked birches waved from the emerald slopes as the foaming white waterfalls went by. Birdsong sounded from the air, feathers brushed the treetops, and graceful hooves clicked on the stones. The mountains leant back to enjoy the sight of a lived-in fjordside. However, they soon sat up again and paid attention: small clearings appeared in the forests, the cliffs echoed with the sound of stone axes, and smoke curled from the hearths of the first houses. Eggshell coracles bobbed on the waves; in time they grew to great boats - the Vikings' elegant dragonships, sailing the fjords on their way to exploration and conquest in the western seas. Indeed, the word "fjord" is derived from "to fare". Through most of the Viking Age the heart of the country was here in the fjords. Nature was stern and aloof, not liking too many children in her skirts; a bad year or two, and the ships set sail and looked for somewhere else to live along the coastal rim, or out at sea among new and unknown lands - Iceland, Greenland and even "Vinland", that is to say, Canada.

Fjords are everywhere in Norway, from Oslofjorden round to Varangerfjorden near the Russian border. Many are long and steep-sided and impressive, it is true, but others are a bit sloppy and even rather dull. The real fjord country, wild and troll-ridden, the landscape that sounds like a shrill Hardanger fiddle, is westwards-looking, from Stavanger in the south to Ålesund in the north. Here are sights which are hardly equalled anywhere else in the world. All right, there are fjords other places as well, but none of them, for all their wildness and drama, have house-room for human beings as well. Nowhere else are there tales of men who built their homes high up the overhanging hillsides, where they had to be as sure-footed as goats to reach their neighbours. But such a life had its advantages too - when the tax-collector came calling, all they had to do was coil up the rope ladder on the steepest cliff, and the authorities had to go home with their tails between their legs.

The southernmost outpost of the fjord realm is also one of the steepest and bleakest, where naked cliffs of polished rock loom high over the fjord. We are, of course, talking about Lysefjorden, a 45 kilometre waterway whose bottom is 450 metres below the shadowed surface. Except that at the entrance, the ice went home early after its demolition job and left a threshold only 13 metres under the waves. The square-cut and polished Prekestolen (Pulpit Rock), nearly 600 metres vertically above the water, is the unrivalled number one attraction in this part of the world. A couple of hours' walk takes you to the flat top of the rock, like a square goat's cheese attached to the mountainside - from which it might at any time split away and plunge into the fjord. Surprisingly enough, more than 50,000 people find their way along the fairly rough trail every year, demonstrating that commercial conspiracies to drill through the rock for express lifts or drape it with chairlifts and God knows what are entirely un- necessary! Not even Norwegian dentists are so industrious as this country's horde of tunnellers and dynamite freaks. Where is the intoxication and feeling of accomplishment in taking a lift from the waves to the 600th floor? Where does that leave the difference between this wonder of gneiss and granite under the open sky and just another of Manhattan's skyscrapers?

Further north in Rogaland we have some smaller fjords like Jøsenfjorden, Saudafjorden and Åkrafjorden, arms about the same length as Lysefjorden but not generally with the same magnificence. By and large the landscape here is gentler, and there is much more habitation along the water's edge.

The next octopus arm on the map is a wide one, and divides like a tree with branches in differ- ent directions. Hardangerfjorden is the second-biggest of Norway's fjords, quite open and smiling and a home for many communities. And to show how they value the fjord, its people have framed it in pink and white May apple-blossom.

Next on the list is Sognefjorden itself, by many called the King of the Fjords, but I would rather say Queen - as beautiful and serene, wild and temperamental as only a woman can be. Three hundred long kilometres of Norwegian lacework, with cross-stitching and back-stitching in every direction: Fjærlandsfjorden, Lusterfjorden, Aurlandsfjorden and Nærøyfjorden itself - the narrowest and most artistic stitch of them all.

Nordfjord, a stone's throw further north, ends with fingers just as splayed as Sognefjorden's. Gently rounded slopes with green pasturelands follow the fjord right up to its headwaters. But if we take a few steps further, and climb a few metres above sea level, we meet the prototype Western Norwegian landscape - Loen and Olden, two valleys enclosed by uprearing mountains, shining snowy peaks and mysterious blue crevasses.

The terminus of our little voyage through the fjord country is Storfjorden, with its tributaries Hjørundfjorden and Synnulvsfjorden. These in turn have their own branches, Norangsfjorden and Geirangerfjorden respectively. This is where the first fjord tourists came, more than a hundred years ago, enjoying the view from the decks of their new-fangled steamboats. Not much has changed since then. The Sunnmøre Alps still dance their reels in their white dresses against a pale blue spring sky and admire their reflections in Norangsfjorden. And Geirangerfjorden with its seven sisters of waterfalls and its famous eagle's-nest farms lives its life still, between pregnant mist-clouds and searchlight sunshine - as it always has done.

In Nærøyfjorden's close embrace, the boats bump their bows on currents fleeing from the glacier above, but there is also room for green lungs and human beings.

You can reach the ends of the earth on a lie,
but you can't get back again.

ANONYMOUS

A horizontal waterfall of large wet snowflakes against blue-grey water, and a sudden searchlight sweeping over Synnulvsfjorden, at the entrance to Geiranger.
And the long, breathless, pastel morning over Aurlandsfjorden, slowly coming alight, even in minus 15°C. This is the fjord country's winter secret.

A painting is a poem without words.

CONFUCIUS

A classic that never fails. Hjørundfjorden is as enticing and dramatic now as the day the first fjord tourists came a hundred years ago.

A life is a glimpse between two eternities.

ANONYMOUS

The mountainside farms, living memorials to strong men and women living in a tough landscape.
Otternes, the cliffside hamlet in Aurlandsfjorden, and Kjeåsen in Eidfjord with its dizzying view,
are both places which you almost have to have cloven hooves to reach.
They make the sea of flowers in Strandebarm, Hardangerfjorden, look like fenland.

It is not just roses that bloom at Rosendal. On mild May days the apple blossom makes a brilliant show against the pink carpets of lady´s smock.
But we have to wait for the clear days of August and September to find out whether the apple trees have done their job.

The may-blossoms of life are never seen again.

SCHILLER

Sailing into Fjærlandsfjorden is like stepping into the Hall of Mirrors at Versailles.
At the end the King contemplates his court from the throne of the Supphellebreen glacier arm.
Lustrafjorden is another copycat: two fishermen become four, and a thousand flowers become two thousand.

THE OCEAN REALM

The ocean is the highway
by which peoples and cultures came and went.
The ocean is a friend, but a capricious sort of friend.
One moment it serves up silver-scaled food on everyone's plate,
the next it furiously drags you down in a frothing rage.
Far out to sea there are huge and incomprehensible forces,
not just cold figures like wind-speed and current,
but magical powers and lost paradises.

*T*he ocean realm is where the land meets this cruel, fickle and smiling sea, the narrow strip between heights and depths that has been the very backbone of Norway's development.

From a distance, our little globe looks bright and blue. If you look closely you can see some green, brown, grey and white too, but the main colour is a rich blue. More than 70% of this wonder of the universe is covered by the azure sea, containing more than 97.5% of all the world's water, or 1,370 million cubic kilometres. And praise be, our globe circles the sun at about 150 million kilometres; not too far, not too near, not too hot, not to cold - just the right distance for the ocean to be where and what it is.

We have the ocean to thank for our being alive. It was here that life began to develop about three thousand million years ago, this is the source of all the fresh water that circulates on the globe, and it is here in the fathomless waters that we find the phytoplankton that produces the oxygen on which we and all other living beings are utterly dependent.

Norway bobs about at the edge of this world-ocean, like a slightly bent arm with a mitten on it, dangling from a shoulder in the northern ice. People with a head for figures have concluded that this ocean realm is a 21,189-kilometre long necklace of mountain teeth that daily chew on the ocean and are chewed in turn. Is Mother Norway spawning out there? For what else should we think when we see the myriads of islands and skerries, islets and holms and cliffs? They break the surface of the sea from one end of the ocean realm to the other, scattered around as if from a violently shaken pepperpot. If we count all the nooks and crannies and the extra shoreline these give, our coastline becomes 54,984 kilometres. Not quite enough to reach the Moon, but a good start!

Here is infinite space, an ocean of time that flows free and untrammelled by our own notions. Co-existence between sea and land is a love-hate relationship that can never be settled by divorce lawyers. We see whispering waves affectionately stroking the cheeks of land; we see temper tantrums in which the sea attacks the shore, tries to climb the highest cliffs and crush the land with the weight of its anger. When there comes a darkness at noon, and a great broom sweeps the land, brushing everything loose under the green carpet, when the Midgard Serpent bellows in the deeps and blows white geysers towards the sky - even then, the land wins in the end, and the crestfallen ocean must slink back, foaming and frothing, to Iceland and Greenland.

Or at least, that is the way it looks to us short-lived and impatient beings. On the long view, it is the sea that has the upper hand, where it grinds and polishes delicate slabs to its own erotic dreams or shoots marbles on the long moraine beaches. It calls on its ally the wind, shovels the sand back and forth and invents new landscapes. It chisels out coves from the hard granite and makes a home for flocks of feathered fishermen who need no nets or lines. Or it piles up middens of kelp and seaweed on the beaches and sows seeds of sea-pink with gardeners' green fingers. Even if it has a violent temper, the sea takes good care of the land....

It was along the coastal rim of the ocean realm that human beings first found their footing, it was here the ice withdrew fastest and here there was enough food. In all probability certain areas of land were ice-free throughout the last Ice Age, new finds in Finnmark show human habitation more than 10,000 years ago. The ocean realm is long, and has many faces. It has moulded its inhabitants more than they have shaped the land.

The south-coaster, the *sørlending*, is as round as soft as his dialect, pleasant and relaxed with all the time in the world for himself and others. No one gets high blood pressure from living in a white south-coast house, from looking over a shoreline of smooth and gentle rocky slabs and rowing out into the sound to catch a mackerel for dinner. You get a sharper profile with the west-coaster, the *vest-lending*, who lives under the abrupt cliffs of Cape Stad. He is used to the Kraken roaring, hammering on the kitchen door and threatening to take the roof and table away with him. This sort of thing makes you a bit cautious and reserved, perhaps a bit tetchy and impatient as well. The *trønder*, from the two Trøndelag counties, is robust and steadfast, just like his flat landscape, and allows no one to put him out of countenance. And the arctic northerner, the *nordlending* - he is simply a separate race that is difficult to classify, just like the landscape of the High North. Fierce and idyllic, steep and flat, hot and cold all at the same time. Perhaps he is a sort of cross between the *vestlending* and the *trønder*. The northerner is harder and tougher than anyone else, he keeps going after others have given up. He has had no choice but to be frugal, but at the same time he is open, generous and hospitable, with a sense of humour that punctures everyone's pretensions.

A voyage through the ocean realm from south to north is a voyage through fierce fates and dramatic events, through stories of trials and sacrifices, but also prosperity and rejoicing. The ocean realm has moulded its inhabitants and their mentality, they have found explanations for the forces and the caprice of nature and organised their lives in the best interests of both.

The islands were one of the most important stimuli to wonder and imagination. Why did they lie just where they were, a joy to their inhabitants but a danger to shipping? It was the trolls who had put them there, usually as a result of a quarrel, or in their pursuit of some nymph or other. For example, the islands of the Oslofjord were made when the King of Ekeberg lost his temper and threw his wife, bag and baggage, into the fjord. As for the Helgeland coast, there were many trollish dances in the old days. One night the Lofoten troll Vågekallen was out courting, he wanted the Leka Maiden *(Lekamøya)* for his wife. She didn't want him, and threw down everything she had in her hands - she was baking at the time - and fled southwards to Leka. The same light summer night the Seven Sisters were out dancing, and they too were frightened and ran away when Vågekallen thundered through the land in his seven-league boots. The Horseman *(Hestmannen)* shot an arrow after him, which went right through the hat of another troll. But when the hue and cry was at its height the first sunbeams topped the horizon and turned all the trolls to mountains in the middle of the sea. The Trolls' Hat *(Trollhatten)* is still there today, hole and all, while Lekamøya ended up all the way down at Leka. The Seven Sisters are still lined up prettily to watch the comedy from their dress circle above Sandnessjøen.

The most intriguing parts of the folk imagination, however, were the islands that you couldn't see at all, the kingdoms of the *huldra*, the paradise islands of the fairy folk, which hovered far from shore between sea and sky - the Norwegian answer to Atlantis. Both Sandflesa and Utvega are well known *huldra* kingdoms, but the most haunted of all is Utrøst - some tens of miles further out than Røst, but no one knows where....

Many a shipwrecked Lofoten fisherman is said to have been saved out there. Isak from Værøy, for example. He was sailing right out to sea when the weather turned, storm and darkness making south into north and east into west. Suddenly the boat touched land, in a glittering realm of plenty, a Cockaigne of waving corn and full nets. Isak was well-received and joined the inhabitants on their eminently successful fishing-trips. He also accompanied the king of that realm to Bergen, and he sold so much fish that he could buy his own sloop. And this sloop was so hallowed by the Unseen that she could never founder, however bad the weather. Isak later found his way back to the kingdom, simply by following the cormorants when they headed out to sea. For the cormorants were the sons of the King of Utrøst.

If we credit the fantastic accounts of the Moskenes "Maelstrom" circulated from the Middle Ages onward (not forgetting Captain Nemo), there are no more dramatic and dangerous waters in the entire world. Between the south cape of Moskenes in Lofoten and the small island of Mosken, there is supposed to be a maelstrom so strong that the earth quakes, whales and ships are whirled round and swallowed up, and the waves rise as high as the mountains.

Of course there were trolls behind it all. The *Værøymannen* and the *Moskeneskjerringa* had this stretch of sea as their communal cookpot, which they both stirred - in opposite directions. The current was said to be particularly dangerous at full moon, for then the old woman was reminded of the moon-lit night her husband went and flirted with the Seven Sisters!

The ocean realm is free, huge and mighty. And who has the heart to stay in bed a bracing autumn morning, when the Creator lights the fire before breakfast? "Jæren - cloud cover, thickening to rain in the afternoon".

Today is the tomorrow you dreamt about yesterday.

CHINESE PROVERB

Time goes by - or not, as the case may be. While the oil capital's helicopters flit and buzz a few miles away,
the old boat and its boathouse lie on the rocky shores of Jæren
- just the way they did when busy people travelled by pony and trap.

A beam of evening light rests peacefully on Kitty L. Kielland's painting from Hå.
Then it goes out. The Kvassheimrauden light is lit instead.

If you cannot lift the stone, let it lie.

NORWEGIAN PROVERB

When the winter storms and snow-showers whip up the sea around Stadlandet,
it isn't easy to stand upright on Norway's West Cape. But what a view of the bays and coves!

Kannesteinen Rock at Måløy is preparing for the worst under a sky as dense as concrete.
Despite this, it rises so elegantly from the sea that Norway's premier sculptor Gustav Vigeland would have been flattered to sign it.

*A cynic is a man who knows the price of everything
and the value of nothing.*

OSCAR WILDE

Fish and fisheries are the theme tune of the ocean realm.
While the fishermen at Veidholmen, Smøla, get ready for the Finnmark season,
the Titran fishing hamlet on Frøya is sunning itself and reminiscing about the old days.
At Nordbotn on Fjellværøya, Hitra, the church is floodlit only by its employer.

The world has enough for human need,
but not human greed.

M.K. GANDHI

A bird darts restlessly over the azure shoreline in the spray from the ocean Mixmaster.
Then the mixture suddenly stiffens, and the wind remembers another job it has to do at Kvalsundet.
But look what it has squirted over the kitchen table!

*The classics should be read in winter,
for then you are better able to concentrate your thoughts.
History should be read in the summer, for then you have the most time.
Read the old philosophers in the autumn, for their thoughts are so charming,
and read the new authors' collected works in the spring,
for then nature reawakens.*

CHANG CHAO

The day dawns at Nykvåg in the Vesteraalen islands; the curlew trills between the mountains and scouts around out to sea.
It sees the grampus enjoying a bubble-bath under the foggy rocks around the Moskenes maelstrom,
while the puffin admires the view from its balcony ledges on the Røst cliffs.

Freedom and life are one.

NORDAHL GRIEG

In Lofoten both premier and king must play second fiddle. Here it is the cod that is absolute ruler.
Does the fellow with the Van Dyke beard down there in the deeps know that Reine and Henningsvær are all his own work?

Grytøya near Harstad greets the fresh, sharp spring sunlight,
while the fishing-smack on the Lyngenfjord thinks that the panorama a bit too strong.
It has used the india-rubber on its surroundings and lies contently bobbing in its own world of damp cotton-wool.

This is the way the ocean realm left the primeval forces' lathe, and at Ekkerøy in the Varangerfjord, nothing much has changed since then.

*It is the diversions and delays
and blind alleys that enrich one's life.*

NILS KJÆR

The snow-showers sweep over Sandfjorden at the outermost edge of the Varanger peninsula's harsh Arctic landscape.
The colourful lichen is one of the few signs of life. Even on a summer's day it is bleak at North Cape, where the world ends.

When the goal is reached,
no one regrets the trouble and effort of the journey.

ARISTOTLE

At the end of March the kittiwakes sail in from the sea and scratch their backs against the blue skies.
After bed and breakfast in the Ekkerøy skyscraper hotel, they stretch their wings again and think about moving in here for good.

Time has his wings on his back
- you don't see them until he has flown past.

HENRIK WERGELAND

Right at the other end of the country Lindesnes Light rests on its polished cliff, like a winking seagull.

We are all living under the same sky,
but not all of us have the same horizon.

KONRAD ADENAUER

In the winter the waves snarl and snap and foam at the mouth - and their spittle freezes on the rocks.
When the beaches of rolling rocks at Mølen in Vestfold look like heaps of glass marbles,
and the Hvaler slabs become dragons' heads with icy breath, the boatsman who knows what's good for him stays at home.

Chisel good deeds in marble - write insults in the sand.

CHINESE PROVERB

Lazy waves playing tag with the light between sea-polished slabs.
This is the southern yachtsmen's dream of summer - made real at Dirhue at Tjøme, Vestfold.

On hot summer days the gently sloping slabs at the "World's End" bathing-place at Tjøme see many attractive curves in a softer material...
In the evenings they try to copy what they have seen. How about a little female torso in the twilight?

Poems should be windows, not mirrors.

ANONYMOUS

THE FOREST REALM

The forest realm is the world of quiet dreams.
In the forest you can hear your own thoughts.
Here are no thundering mountains,
roaring waves or switchback plateaux under an infinite sky.
In the empire of the trees everything is within reach,
floor and walls are an arm's length away.
Just by turning slowly round you will see more, smell more
and feel more than if you walked five miles
in the high mountains or sailed five miles at sea.
The forest is an intimate realm,
where you can take possession of billions of pine-needles, ants,
mosses and tufts of grass without moving from the spot.

*Y*ou go <u>into</u> the forest, into the busy kingdom that gently forms itself to fit the ridges and valleys. You are shut into a room where you feel at home, you are on the same wavelength as the carrion beetles that carry off the dead mouse, you greet the blueberries that make the world's best pancake filling, you talk to the black woodpecker, which according to legend is an old baker-woman. The forest is a sociable place where everyone knows everyone else. The voices of the birds rise up between the arboreal crowns and carry messages between the trees like schoolchildren slipping notes between the desks. No footsteps echo on stone and slabs, but sink soundlessly into the soft green, over rotting trunks and glittering streams that babble and sing. You don't miss the starry sky or the flare of the Northern Lights, but see the macrocosm reflected in the microcosm of the forest floor.

When the mist seeps through the trees and the twilight falls, you feel eyes on the back of your neck, or scrutinising your face. You see shadows crouching down behind trees and rocks. Branches snap in fright when a ghostly moose ambles between the trunks. The fairy folk dance behind trees covered in old-man's-beard, the Aeolian harp plays in the forest canopy, and Pan sounds his pipes at the gates of dawn. When the sun casts its first javelins through the morning mist and surrounds the upthrust roots of fallen trees in a blaze of glory, the world stops in its tracks, and you feel an urge to go further and further into the haunted forest to come face to face with whatever is calling you - gnome or troll, sprites or nymphs. If there is any landscape that seems to stretch the boundaries of reality, it is the forest...

In most cultures and most religions the life force is symbolised by a tree. Our Norse version, Yggdrasil, is only one example of the World-Tree that embraces and unifies the cosmos. When the tree falls, it is the Twilight of the Gods and the end of the world.

Our forefathers had great respect for trees. Large and beautiful trees were valuable vessels of vital forces, perhaps especially if they grew in a farmyard, on a barrow or other man-made places. Cutting down such giants would bring bad luck. The barn brownie lived here, and he was normally a benevolent fellow who looked after "his" humans; he spent a lot of time in the stable and byre taking care of the animals. But he liked to be left in peace, and every now and then, particularly at Christmas and other festivals, he liked to be given some treats. A little porridge and a little ale was all it took to keep him cheerful. There are plenty of tales of people who came to a new place and neglected to set out some tasty morsels for the brownie. He soon made his feelings known, for example by lifting the house from the foundations or whipping up a storm. This was generally enough to remind the farmer of his manners. But if the new tenant cut down the tree for firewood, disasters would queue up to afflict the farm, and it generally ended by falling very quickly into rack and ruin. Sometimes, however, the bond of fate was so strong that even when the tree toppled in the natural way, the farm would slowly but surely fail. Other places it was even worse: if the tree fell, the whole world would follow.

Those who worked in the forest often saw *huldra* herding their brindled cows with braided tails, they saw ghosts and spectres. If a tree was remarkable in some way, like a fir with three trunks in one story, no one would dare to cut it down. The tough guy who finally tried it was struck dead by a chip right in the brows. If a jay flew by when the lumberers were setting out, they would turn round and go straight home again - there was no end to what could go wrong otherwise. The shaft of the axe might break, at great hazard to hands and fingers. For the jay had fairy blood.

The Ice Ages were very effective erasers. Our great subtropical forests of deciduous and coniferous trees were utterly wiped out and the landscape's calendar was reset at Day One. 10,000 years ago was a new beginning, with blank pages and new green crayons. Slowly but surely the forest as we know it today took form. The first colonists were the hardy dwarf birch and osiers, and hard on their heels came the birchwood. Soon the evening light began to play the sunbeam organ on proud and stubborn pine-trunks. Increasing warmth summoned hazel, elm, maple and oak. The Entry of the Fir-Trees, however, could not have been played less than a couple of thousand years ago. But when the fir forest came, it came. The entire eastern part of Southern Norway, and Central Norway too, was invaded by fir, while the pines were pushed out to the poor soils and parched cliffs.

It was our Johnny-come-lately fir forest, our little chip of the vast Siberian taiga, that was the birthplace of most of the legends and stories woven into the forest landscape through the centuries. Just like the mycelious network of fungal threads binds the roots of a tree together, the belief was that nature was bound together by human beings and gnomes, brownies and wood-nymphs in a respectful community.

That was then and this is now. The trolls, nymphs, sprites and gnomes have vanished from the great forests. No more do you hear the axe of the woodman who knows and loves his trees. Our forests have become lumber factories in which the chain-saw screams, the chains rattle and the timber-trucks thunder. The realm of axe, bark-knife and one horsepower has become the battlefield of steel, diesel and turbo-engines, covered with the mutilated corpses of the Norwegian Chain-Saw Massacre. Distances are getting longer and longer between the last remnants of the rich and multifarious forest with its timeless, enclosed spaces. Instead, new trees are planted in close-order formation, just like field crops. Of course there is no room for nymphs and sprites, we would hardly expect that: what is worse is that the less immaterial inhabitants are given their cards too. For example, the moss called *huldrastry*, wood-nymph's yarn, or the Lapp's Tinder fungus on trees, the little wood lemming - or the three-toed woodpecker, the capercaillie and the goshawk. These inhabitants, who had tenanted the forest since the dawn of time, rarely have new homes to move into when their old ones are demolished.

Over the whole forest landscape, moreover, there hangs the same cloud that has destroyed our lakes and rivers - acid rain. The more intact and natural our forests are, the more they can fight back against this dead hand of European industry.

If you want to experience the forest realm of Norway, you should do it now. You still have a lot of opportunities. If you like to take strolls along well-marked paths, you will perhaps be happiest in the Oslomarka, the rolling forests around the capital, and near the other Eastern Norwegian and Trøndelag towns. If you really want to penetrate the forest realms, the Finnskog Trail is just right for you. This trail on the Norwegian-Swedish border takes a week to walk, and will reward you with many experiences. You will be passing through the realm of the bear and the wolf, and who knows, perhaps this is where the last *huldras* are hiding, with their beautiful faces, braided hair and cow's tails.....

If you don't want to follow in the steps of other humans, but would prefer to create your own path in pristine virgin forest and green mossy bogs, it is a bit more difficult. Two national parks, Gutulia and Ormtjernkampen, can offer untouched primeval woodland. They are pearls, but far too small. There are also a number of forest reserves scattered about, but some of the finest patches of virgin forest, with rare species and prehistoric atmosphere, are still holding their breath in the shadow of the forest-rapists and their gigantic machinery.

The big surprise is ready for opening - Father Sun chases the dancing sprites away from the surface - and the package of colours is opened.

The world is a beautiful book,
but useless to the man who cannot read.

CARLO GOLDONI

A leaden heaven parts the way for the evening sun after dropping its load of November snow.
Next morning you don't have to be Sherlock Holmes to know what the hare has been up to.

Truth is a diamond whose rays take many paths.

GOETHE

Some trees are good rock-climbers, others are not.
The birch is a born Alpinist who clambers right up to the bare mountain along the banks of Vangsmjøsa,
while a bit further down the slopes there is more variety and a wider range of colours. In the dramatic stonescape
of the Giant's Cut *(Jutulhogget)* in Reindalen. it is the pines that plant the flag.

The outermost pines on Jeløya, Østfold, stand like tin soldiers shivering on parade in a merciless wind.
In rather more sheltered areas crystals glitter from frozen fogbanks, until the snow is packed tight around the gnarled feet of the trees.

In spring the young tree shouts with joy,
but the forest falls silent under the weight of snow.

ARNULF ØVERLAND

The forest can be the country of dreams, even in the Oslomarka round the capital.
As when the midwinter sun tries to illuminate the dense stands of fir at Spålen, Nordmarka,
or autumn mists drift between clumps of bog whortleberries and fir trunks in the Østmarka forest preserve.

The spring woods are full of chuckling and trilling voices.
Rivers and streams are a merry company and capercaillies' courting glades quiver with ancient, magical forces.
Further into the wilds, in the last redoubt of the primeval forest giants,
Father Bear lumbers about with a torn hide after a recent meeting with a rival.

There is none so blind as he who does not wish to see.

ITALIAN PROVERB

The forest is more than birch, pine and fir.
The matchstick aspens that fence Sperillen lake will eventually become a "des.res." for black woodpecker families.
And the ruby clusters of the mountain ash make a cordon bleu dinner for restless thrushes.

THE REALM OF MOUNTAINS

They have just been there, the mountains, as long as we can recall.
The high plateaux, gently undulating
like a sea of rock in a light breeze, and with a roof so high
that you look the Creator in the eye every time you fall
gratefully into the grass after a day's walk.
But the mountain realm is not only horizontal lines.
As soon as you have snuggled under the duvet of the plateau landscape
and begun to drop off, you bang your head on the headboard
and stub your toes on the bedframe.
The vertical lines rip the bottom out of the clouds,
looking for the short-cut to the heavens.

*T*his is the mountain realm, a mixture of the horizontal and the vertical. And, fortunately, the diagonal as well - the line old Pythagoras drew between the bottom and the side of the triangle, the line that enables us poor mortals to reach the summits without hanging over yawning depths and struggling like fish on the line.

"United and faithful until Dovre falls" was the oath of the Fathers of the Norwegian Constitution. For them the mountains were the symbol of the eternal. But the memory of man is a short day in the calendar of the mountains. The oldest parts of the fatherland were born in a cauldron of fire between 2.6 and 1 billion years ago; after that they were kneaded and pounded by ice and water, turned over younger sediments like pancakes and pressed down again. Even since the first real Norwegians were born in the cold breath of the great ice-field a mere 10,000 years ago, the mountains have changed, become slimmer and sharper or flatter and more comfortable. How can these little people be so full of themselves, when they have watched only one grain of sand fall through the hourglass?

I wonder whether our forefathers, with their animal skins and bone clubs, gazed their fill at the mountains until they knew every summit, the way we do, and remembered them fondly when the clouds came down or the firelight closed the circle? Probably not. Across the abyss of the centuries it was a matter of food, clothes and the other necessities of survival. They may have looked on the mountains only to curse them, because wherever they wanted to go the mountains were in the way. The old tracks ran in every direction, up hill and down dale. Traders shuttled over the Hardanger plateau between the eastern valleys and the western fjords. The old and sick struggled over Dovre to reach St. Olav's healing shrine in Trondheim.

There were no Gore-Tex clothes, anatomical rucksacks and primus stoves in those days. Crossing the mountains was a gamble with life and death when plateaux became featureless voids in snow and cloud, or wind and rain chilled the body until its last sleep. As if the weather was not dangerous enough, the mountains were the habitations of titans, giants, trolls, witches and the rest of the demonic horde. What else but their family quarrels could create such a banging and crashing and wailing and howling as frightened travellers experienced in these wild realms?

Since trolls and other such ill-omened beings always turned to stone in the sunlight or when they encountered holy powers, peaks with strange shapes were usually associated with the supernatural. The trolls that St. Olav turned into stone in Romsdal during his missionary journey are well-known now as the Trolltindane summits - so steep that people jump off them with parachutes. The ogress of Gaustatoppen in Telemark was fond of nocturnal sprees, and one morning she was a little late back. Just as she was creeping into her mountain hall, the sun rose. She burst, of course, and you can still see her ribs today, in the corrugated mountainside where the snow lies in strips far into the summer.

Some mountains are famous for crashing and rumbling whenever the weather is about to change, such as Skotshorn in Valdres and Isflåmannen in Vartdal. People said there was a giant in Skotshorn who coughed when the weather turned, while Isflåmannen was supposed to contain a trapped dragon.

Dovrefjell, Hornelen in Nordfjord and Blåkoll at Bø in Telemark were the most famous witches' parliaments. It was here they gathered on certain days in the year, all evil and demonic powers, and made an infernal din with fighting and rumbling, sulphur, venom and gall. St. Olav cleaned up Hornelen somewhat when he sailed past and turned the local giant to stone. He can still be seen up near the top.

Young girls should stick close to other good Christians and not wander about the wilds alone. For the sinister denizens of the mountain underworld had a mighty appetite for fair damsels. They could either lure them further and further into the forests and mountains with their fiddle-playing - or not bother with such refinement and simply carry them off. The bowels of the mountains would be their home for ever more, bearing sons and daughters for the trolls. The only way to save such bewitched girls - the Norwegian word is "seized into the mountain" - was to ring the church bells loud and long at the gate of the mountain kingdom. The rocks might then open and let the girl out. But even if she was freed, she would never be the same again....

Nowadays only the coldest and most inhospitable parts of the mountain landscape are white with glaciers. The country's robe of ice is tattered and torn - into nearly 1600 bits to be precise, perhaps as a supply of ice-cubes for the giants' cocktails (aquavit on the rocks, of course). And if the mountains in themselves were grim and frightening for our forefathers, these crevassed and treacherous glaciers were the worst revenge the supernatural forces could wreak on humanity. Folgefonna, for example, was created as a punishment for the people of the fertile Folgedalen. They were so ungodly complacent that the Almighty grew weary of them and let it snow for ten weeks without pause. When it stopped the valley, with all its seven parishes of people, was completely buried under a dome of snow and ice. And legend has it that Svartisen, Norway's second-biggest icefield, was made by the Sami king of Misvær to block the way of St. Olav as he advanced northwards, converting the country to Christianity. Four women, a newly-baptised mother and her three daughters, are said to have perished on Jostedalsbreen when they fled to Mundal. There was such a terrible storm with thunder and lightning that they were turned to stone, and can still be seen atop Norway's biggest icecap.

Modern people have liberated themselves from Nature's hard grasp, shaken off the belief in trolls and sprites and forgotten much of their own history. Thanks to individuals like J.J. Rousseau, the national-romantic painters and the folklore collectors, we have come to have a more positive attitude to the mountains. They have become a place for freedom, experiences, self-examination - and tired feet. We walk and ski in the mountains simply because we like it, we see peaks putting their golden hats on in the morning and taking them off at night without wondering whether trolls or other evil beings live in them. We enjoy the clear voices of bluethroats and becks, and broad eagles' wings circling above the cliffs. We have conveniently-spaced cabins and lodges overflowing with provisions, and we can buy all kinds of aids and equipment. Is it strange, then, that we can enjoy a trip "out into the Nature", when we can drive so conveniently to the trailhead and the only place we are likely to meet dangerous predators is on the television?

Thank heaven that we still have wide swathes of mountain scenery to flee to, now that life is almost too easy to be lived. But whatever happens, let us not make the mountain walk into an experience just as superficial as a soap opera or tabloid headlines. We may be thankful that the bad old days are gone, but should we not try to conjure up some of the old respect for the land and for nature, the reverence that underlies the legends, myths and superstitions? Let us combine the best of the old and the best of the new, let mind and soul be filled with new knowledge, wonder and respect. Our mountain expeditions will then be something more than sporting feats or collection of extra food for the table.

The mountain realm is half the size of Norway. No other of our various landscapes can boast such dimensions. It is a spartan realm, with few facilities for greedy humans. For this reason it has been left in peace to a greater degree than the rest of the country. Even if hydro schemes, roads, cabins and mines have left their many scars, our biggest and most important national parks are also to be found in the mountains. The mountain realm still contains enough variety for a long life's wandering.

The Hardanger Mountain Plateau is southern Norway's biggest amphitheatre for restless herds of wild reindeer and well-shod humans. In Jotunheimen and on the edge of the western ocean rise spiky peaks frosted with glaciers. In the east is Rondane's refined and shapely kingdom around the foot of Rondeslottet; further north it gives way to Norway's national symbol, Dovre. In Central Norway the country relaxes for a bit, with the gentler ranges of Sylane and Gressåmoen on the Swedish border. After that the pearls are close together on the string: Okstindane, the Sulitjelma range, Rago National Park, and the unbelievable Lofoten islands, which have been compared to the Chamonix Aiguilles with water up to the neck. In the furthest north the landscape settles down once more; the whole of Finnmark county is a huge plateau that rolls to the rim of the world at North Cape - and over the edge.

Between Jostedalen's austere and precipitous mountainsides, a sudden green oasis.
Here the fairy-tale princess can go out at midnight to gather soft cotton-grass for her knitting.

The greatest luxury in life is loneliness
- all you have to do is furnish it with the inner life.

HENRI MATISSE

The weather is a moody walking-companion in the summer mountains. Sun and rain, light and shadow in the same minute,
lending the landscape life and drama - and there is always shelter to find!
The Arctic fox in the Sylane mountains disappears into his earth when the showers come,
while the Gaularfjell bothies look after the two-legged traveller.

Bare mountains? Far from it. In the autumn the plants are all colour-coded,
and so you can see how many voices go to make the motet sung in Døråldalen at the foot of the Rondane massif.

Nature appeals to us when it seems to be Art
- Art when it seems to be Nature.

IMMANUEL KANT

Teodor Kittelsen's troll-pack don't mind if the sun is shining *behind* the Trysil mountains, but are petrified with horror if the light reaches *them*. Then human beings can safely walk abroad without being seized and carried into the mountains.

When you have walked so far that you feel you cannot walk another step,
you have walked half as far as you can.

GREENLAND PROVERB

Never before have I seen such a heavenly spectacle as on this winter afternoon in Storlidalen, Trollheimen.
Was it a wing of UFOs training for the invasion up there in the stratosphere?

I close my eyes with the blessed knowledge
that I have left a ray of light upon the earth.

LUDWIG VAN BEETHOVEN

A hint of winter has sugared Sognefjell. The unreal-seeming lunar landscape with its cracked skin is rawer and fiercer than ever before
- more monumental and unapproachable for tiny humans.

In nature, mountains loom - at home, the bagatelles.

EIVIND BERGGRAV

The winter night is long and cold in the High North, as here under the overwhelming majesty of the Lyngsalpene.
It is good to warm yourself in the "lavvu", as the Sami people have done from time immemorial.
The audience has a long wait before the Northern Lights' laser-light show begins in the amphitheatre.

Do not stand under the stars and complain that there is no light in your life.

HENRIK WERGELAND

Man is the only animal that feels shame - or has reason to.

MARK TWAIN

Reindeer and musk-ox, the first inhabitants of a Norway freshly emerged from the ice and snow.

Every year many people pass the Roof of Norway, Jotunheimen, and its highest peak Glittertind.
But few get to see the symphony of colour when the first pink brush touches the rim of the glacier and the serried row of peaks
at an ungodly hour of an August morning...

I will go further, higher, to the steepest peak
- I will see the sun rise once more.

HENRIK IBSEN

Nobody can spend a Lofoten midsummer night at the edge of the world without being refreshed to the roots of his soul.
If you have once seen the blue mountains pull the soft duvets over their heads in their pink bedrooms,
you will never again worry about the unimportant things.

What can you own, when life itself is a loan?

ARNULF ØVERLAND

As if formed by a glass artist, the glacier`s immense ice masses slide down the mountainside.
A cold, blue and unreal world confronts us insignificant beings.

If you do not climb the mountain, you cannot see the valley.

CHINESE PROVERB

THE WATER REALM

A drop of water. A quivering, delicate drop
hanging at the very tip of an equally trembling and delicate straw.
So small and insignificant, but nevertheless embracing a whole world.
Bend down, and you will see the earth in there, upside down.
A landscape with green trees and lush grass,
running animals and singing birds. And people.
Water is life, for both the landscape and its creatures.
Just as sap flows in plants and blood in animals,
water flows as rivers and streams across the earth - a fresh, bubbling liquid
that brings oxygen and nourishment,
and carries away the remains of the meals the cells have eaten.

*W*ater. For the chemist a simple compound of hydrogen and oxygen. For the philosopher and anthroposophist a separate source of life, perhaps the most important of all elements; a liquid with memory, energy and soul. When it flows freely in large or small vessels, it has its own inner motion, its own life, which gives as much energy and vigour to its surroundings as it can. The molecules proceed in swinging spirals, alike in both the broadest of rivers and the smallest of capillaries.

In the beginning was Nothing. Only the primal void, that the Norsemen called "Ginnungagapet". But three strong forces were at work, from three springs. On the one side cold, on the other side heat, and between them the deepest and greatest - the well-spring of wisdom. Yggdrasil, the World-Tree, the ash that spreads its boughs over the whole earth, grows with a root in each of these springs. In the cold spring, the Well of Hvergelmir, is the art of living and the power of endurance. In the hot Urdabrunnr the gods keep house and gather to create justice on the earth. Here are also the bright goddesses, the Valkyries, swimming in the clear water in the form of swans. The Well of Wisdom is in the land of the Jotuns, the Giants. It is guarded by Mimir, who himself drinks from it and is wiser than all others. When Balder was dead and Odin despaired of the world and its future, he went to Mimir to share his wisdom. "Hmm", said Mime, "First give me a sign that you really want clarity of thought!" Odin tore out one of his eyes and threw it into Mimir's well. Odin received his wisdom and the world was saved.

Two seeds of Yggdrasil sprouted and became the first human beings the world had seen: Ask and Embla. Their children were nourished on the water from the three wells, they grew up strong and vital, creative and wise.

If the wells dry up, the Tree will wither, and Ragnarok, the Twilight of the Gods, will be at hand. But the day the water in the well of wisdom reaches its former level, the world will rise once more from the ocean.

Thus the Icelandic Eddas on the origin of the world: poetry and the wisdom of life in harmonious union.

Sorcery or the miracles of God, all ages have found something magical in the clear and pure springs, where water suddenly and quite unannounced decides to gush forth from the bowels of the earth. There must have been strong forces at work where the earth opens and the water of life runs out. Perhaps the forest gods, gnomes or trolls had been abroad, or perhaps the holy powers in their struggle with evil. If the water runs from the source northwards, there is extra magic in it. For the North is the home of all evil powers, all demons, trolls and ogresses who cannot abide the smell of Christian blood. Such a north-running spring was thought to have particularly strong healing powers; its water could draw out from the body the evil that created the sickness and send it to the north where it belonged.

After the introduction of Christianity the sources were "taken over" by holy powers. They were named for saints, usually Norway's patron St. Olav, and became the goals of pilgrimages. They had extra power on the Eve of St. John, Midsummer Night. Children were baptised where possible in spring water, for in baptism the small, perhaps devil-possessed beings would be freed from evil powers and enter the Kingdom of God. They were born again by being immersed three times in the brimming baptismal font.

While the groundwater is hidden and only reveals itself to the few chosen ones in the sources' magical watery "eyes", surface water is something that is not hard to find in Norway. There are more than 210,000 lakes and tarns in Norway, not counting all the small boggy pools. So many, but no two alike. Some are round, some oval, others long as intestines, branching, bent or curling back on themselves. A master-joiner's nightmare, to be commissioned to make frames for such odd-shaped mirrors! Fortunately, however, these mirrors need no other frames than the ones they already have. Elegant firs surround the mirrors, dip their branches to the surface in curiosity and admire their reflections. The mountains are prouder and cast only a quick glance over their shoulders from their commanding heights. But they too like what they see.

The realm of water. This is a world of riches and variety, a parliament of water-sprites and wood-nymphs, elves and fairies. Nymphs' double-bottomed pools that cheat the fisherman; only churchyard soil scattered in a circle around the pool will keep the Unseen at bay and allow the fish to be landed.

The realm of water: mornings with the mist lifting gently off the lake, when the world is bundled into soft forms, and the circles where the fish come up to feed become golden saucers in the first rays of the sun. The beaver takes the last patrol of the night shift and the moose splashes through the bog with water-lilies in the corners of his mouth.

The realm of water is mountain plateaux undulating in the evening light, with a glittering jewel in every little hollow.

And then there are the rivers and waterfalls. The nerves of the landscape, descending like escalators from floor to floor, to end up where the water began its round dance - the great world ocean. Innumerable lakes and rivers in combination with high and steep mountains: this has made Norway the land of waterfalls second to none. In the giddy days of a West Norwegian May you can hear water trickling, chuckling, singing and thundering down every mountainside. Statistics show that our senses are not deceiving us: of the world's 63 waterfalls with the greatest overall height, 43 are Norwegian!

The waterfall is the kingdom of the Nixie, who plays the violin or harp under the waters. The Nixie is a benevolent fellow, for he likes to take on students. But these must bring a piece of fat and juicy meat for their teacher. There is a story of a boy who threw a half-chewed leg of mutton to the Nixie. He learnt to play all right - but he could never tune his fiddle!

The English name for the black and brown bird with the white tuxedo that spends all its time in close proximity to running water is the "dipper" or "water-ouzel", but its Norwegian name is also another name for the Nixie. It is the very incarnation of the Norwegian folk soul - or at any rate, how the Norwegians like to think of themselves: the tough Viking who stays unaffected by winter and cold and who makes his living anywhere there is a flat patch between the rocks and a little running water, always cheerful. No wonder the dipper has been chosen as Norway's national bird.

The overwhelming power of the waterfall has been a magnet for folk belief, and there is many a legend about the man who jumped across ravines of roaring waters. Either he had his bride in his arms, escaping his enemies; or he was condemned to jump as a penalty for murder or other crimes; or else he was just proving his manhood with deeds of daring.

The waterfalls were viewed with respect as untameable and dangerous powers, and some places doom and disaster was predicted for anyone who dared to insult them by building a bridge. Today we do whatever we want with them, and most of the biggest and finest have either gone for good or are heavily regulated. In order to use four times as much electricity as the average Central European and win the prize for the world's biggest power-gobblers, the Norwegians have killed nearly three-quarters of the country's 43 highest waterfalls (including the world's second and third biggest), while most of the others have much less water to put on their show with.

Other unpleasant facts are that over large areas the lakes, particularly in the southern and eastern parts, are now so acid that many of them cannot support fish. The few fish that try their luck need full overhauling and gill-cleaning once a week. The acidity comes from above, in the form of duty-free and zero-VAT imports from both east and west - part of the new frontierless Europe.

The thirst for power has even changed the geography. Nature meant Femunden to be the country's second-biggest lake, with its 204 km². But then homo sapiens came along and made Rossvatnet in Nordland into a reservoir of 210 km². Even so, Mjøsa is still leading the field at 368 km². And the Glomma is still the country's longest river, flowing all the 611 km between Riasten in the Tydal mountains, through the Østerdalen valley to Fredrikstad.

Roaring masses of water hurl themselves down into a coloursplashed, boiling cauldron at the legendary Vøringfossen waterfall on the edge of the Hardanger mountain platau. Even the boldest shooters of rapids must content themselves with a sideline view of scenes like this, although they are not usually afraid of testing their strength against the watery element.

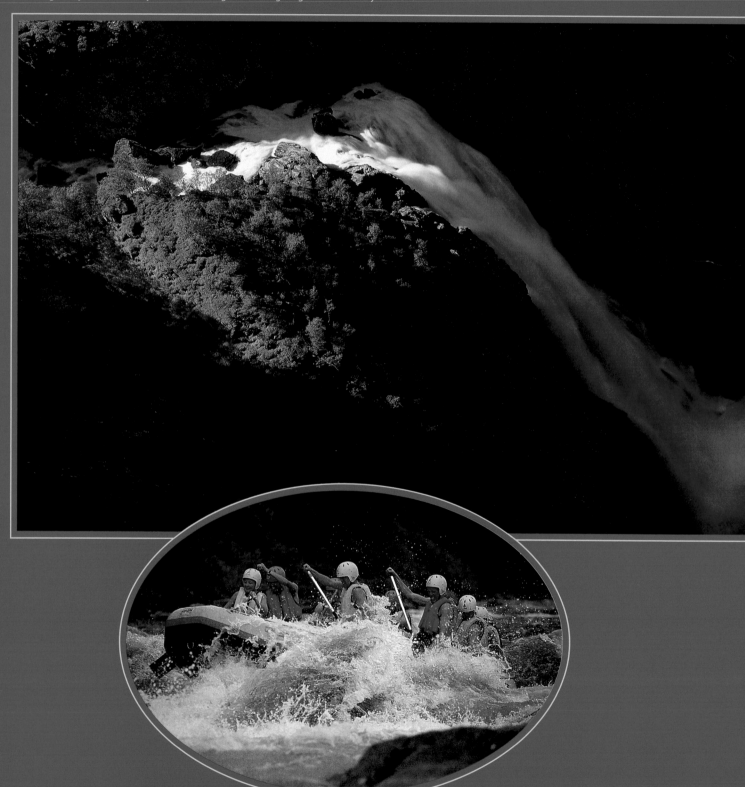

To master Nature you must first obey her.

FRANCIS BACON

The forest stream likes the deep Trysil woods so much that it curls back on itself, unwilling to leave.

A trip with M/V "Victoria" on the Telemark Canal is as much a journey in time as in space.
When the old queen huffs and puffs her way from Dalen wharf via Bandak to Skien, our thoughts go to the setting of local man Henrik Ibsen's dramas.

For the mariner who does not know what port he is steering for,
no winds are favourable.

SENECA

In the delicate mood of a summer's night, the spirit of the pool and the elves put on a command performance
in front of a backcloth painted with the economy and elegance of Japanese brushwork.
The cloth is slowly lowered, and the blue shadow of a moose splashes into our world before vanishing into eternity.

You must rejoice in life every single day,
do not wait until it is past until discovering that it was good!
Do not place your happiness in the days to come.
The older we get, the more we feel that the enjoyment
of the moment is a state of grace, a golden gift.

MARIE CURIE

THE WATER REALM

Lots of cold and little snow is the recipe for the transformation of Elgåfossen in Østfold into Tarjei Vesaas' Ice Castle.
No one wants to bathe now, so the lake becomes a gallery for modern ice sculpture instead.

The most advanced of all is the simple.

FREDRIK WISLØFF

After a heavy, wet evening comes a cold and clear winter morning.
The panorama island is packed in silk and served for breakfast with delicate frosting.

He who desires the many small rights and freedoms,
will harvest the great wrongs and the worst slavery.

SIGRID UNDSET

THE REALM OF MAN

The realm of Man. Words we can taste carefully, test on the tongue,
suck on and finally swallow. For this is not something that is easy
to grasp or define, and statistics don't help.
Only 0.8% of Norway's surface area is built on, they say,
and 2.8% is cultivated soil. In other words, 96.4%
of the country is uninhabited and unaffected by Man!
Rarely can the facts be so hopelessly wrong. The truth is that
almost wherever you walk, drive or paddle in Norway,
you will see traces of homo sapiens.
With some of these you have to know what you're looking for,
like the animal pits in the forests and on the mountains, or petroglyphs
covered by moss and lichen. Others are all too obvious,
such as the great grainfields round Lake Mjøsa
or the Postgiro Building and Hotel Plaza in Oslo!

*A*lmost all of Norway shows traces of human habitation. So what about the realm of Man, is this everything or almost nothing? We must hurry up and make boundaries around the concept, frame it and hang it where it belongs.

Semi-natural cultivated land, we call it: the landscape where Man has trodden lightly and only cautiously and prudently helped himself to Nature's larder. Here Nature still has the upper hand and can easily rub out Man's line in the guest-book, if she is only allowed some decades of peace and quiet. **Rural landscape** is a half-way house: more human, but changed to a moderate degree and on Nature's premises. **Intensive cultivation** and the **urban landscape** are something else again, both landscape types are fully shaped and reorganised by people, so that Nature has little chance of putting it all back the way it was, even after long and heroic efforts.

It is the rural landscape, and the even more transformed cultivated land, that strikes our eye most. The landscape where fertile soil yields good crops and where the towns fortunately remain small and isolated dots on the map, not running into each other like ink-blots.

The wide, open cultivated landscape is quite a recent invention in Norway. In the last century even the best breadbaskets were a fine mosaic of stream ditches, knolls, bits of woodland and coppices. The landscape was cultivated, to be sure, but not reshaped by human beings. Around the turn of the century, however, they found more and more ways of redesigning the landscape in their own image. Drainage, dynamite and machinery were the thing. Nature's barriers could be surmounted and more food grown for an increasing population. Still, however, the fields had to be manured in the old way, there had to be a balance between cultivated acreage and the number of animals. The crucial leap forward was chemical fertiliser. From then onwards, people could eat nutritious food from artificially-fertilised pastureland and extend the grainlands as much as they liked. Small farms were swallowed up by the large ones, and the machine was king.

The class of crofters or small tenants had no part in this development, they still had to poke around on their tiny patches of land at the edge of the forest and put their animals out to pasture on the commons. This allowed the countryside to retain its multiplicity and variety even in the new age. When the crofters were freed and left the land for the growing towns, the transformation of the agricultural landscape entered its last act.

Dandelion meadows bursting with the joys of spring, golden corn pricking up its ears in the August sun - surely a sign of harmony and fertility? A green and pleasant land, indeed, but still an entirely different picture from a few decades ago. There were not nearly as many dandelions or so dense corn-fields, but instead there were so **many** plants, so **many** shapes and colours. Among the knolls of the upper meadows, now half-grown commercial fir plantations, blossomed the harebell, the caraway, the oxeye daisy, the campion and the sunflower; and here the corncrake sat on its nest in the safe knowledge that the mowers would not arrive before well into July. Here the theme was multiplicity of species, just as in the old fir forest.

In Eastern Norway today there are only a few living reminders of this varied countryside. Western Norway is, fortunately, better-placed. Here it was the untidy geography - a muddle of mountains, rocky tors, wooded hills, fjords and islands - that saved large parts of the rich ecology of the cultivated lands for posterity. In those parts of the country it was simply not possible to reshape the landscape to any great degree. This is why you can still see haymakers swinging the scythe in the steep meadows - where a tractor would immediately tip over - and admire the green pasturelands with their coppiced trees, reminders of a traditional foraging that is still partly kept up.

The "flora" of human contemporary monuments was also reduced and impoverished by the steamroller of Progress. The ancient log cabins of the rich rural landscape, with folk ballads echoing in the rafters, were left to rot where they stood, rejected for breezeblock walls and formica tables. Fortunately some people were more far-sighted than others, and they made sure that valuable buildings were maintained and allowed to stand where they always had - instead of being pickled and pinned in a museum. In Gudbrandsdalen, particularly in the side-valley of Heidal, in Telemark and Setesdal, living farm landscapes have been preserved; large complexes of simple, tarred buildings, older even than the rings of the oldest timber. The creaking of the doors seems to remember Olav Åsteson, Håvard Hedde and Margit Hjukse, heroes of the old oral tradition of folk-tales; old larder-houses balance on their mouse-proof stilts and many pages of the history books are carved into the wood with hunters' knives.

Even more spectacular and magnificent, but in the same sober spirit, is the jewel in our cultural crown - the stave churches. These are houses of worship that, protected by higher powers (and some of us people), have survived plague, war and vandalism all the way from the epoch of the bloodthirsty Vikings. There may have been more than a thousand stave churches originally, today there are only 30 left. Instead of the otherwise usual method of building in horizontal logs, "cogging", the churches' load-bearing components are vertical wooden pillars or "staves". The most famous trinity of stave churches is Heddal (the biggest), Urnes (the oldest) and Borgund (the best-preserved).

The Heddal stave church is a veritable wooden cathedral. It seems too large to have been built by human hand; that is what they thought in the old days, at least, and there is a legend about it. Raud Ryggi was a Heddal farmer who wanted to build a church to the new deity whom the Vikings called the White Christ. A stranger turned up who offered to see to the building. He worked so fast that Raud grew frightened - on only the third day the building was taking shape. For Raud had agreed to meet one of the master-builder's three conditions: he must either fetch the sun and moon down from heaven, let his heart's blood flow, or find out the stranger's name. The faster the building went, the more afraid he became. But then suddenly a voice cried out from a nearby mountain, that in a riddle told Raud that the stranger was called Finn and lived in the mountain. When Raud took over the church and addressed Finn by his right name, the giant disappeared into Lifjellet and banged the door after him!

Through the centuries most Norwegians have lived on scattered farms and eked out a living as smallholders and fishermen. Urban conglomerations have not been part of the soul of the people; towns and their culture were of little significance until industrialisation started in earnest in the 1800s.

A slightly denser population arose primarily where people's lives intersected, at crossroads or ports. This was also the birth of the present big towns, many of which can trace their origins to the Viking Age, about a thousand years ago. In the 1600s and 1700s a couple of towns appeared in the interior, with quite a different history. These were mining communities, built in the wilds to take advantage of ore deposits. At Kongsberg ("The King's Mines") it was the silver glinting in the rock, while Røros was the copper-mining town.

We find some of our cultural heritage preserved in the towns as well: large and magnificent buildings such as the Gothic cathedral in Trondheim and a number of impressive fortifications. In contrast to this architecture of power and glory, we can point to a number of small and intimate urban milieux of old wooden houses. The Hansa Wharf in Bergen, the Hansa merchants' base in the far North, is perhaps the best-known, but also the old garrison town at Frederikstad, the white-painted historic core of Stavanger and not least Røros -where the whole town is a living museum.

Norway has no cities founded by megalomaniac rulers where there was nothing before. Nature and people have decided in partnership where they are to be, and the new arose on the shoulders of the old. This makes for a healthy environment and healthy people!

The Eiffel Tower, the Colosseum and the Taj Mahal - the Norwegian cultural heritage is not as imposing, but it smells better!
When the floodlights reflect from Heddal Stave Church and the work of sculpture that is Borgund Stave Church poses on a May morning,
then there is history in the resinous scent of the pine.

Pass through this little piece of time
in accordance with nature and end your journey with contentment,
as when an olive falls from the tree because it is ripe
and thanks the tree that bore it.

MARCUS AURELIUS

The old Telemark larder-house is a microcosm of history.
Many pages of the history book are concealed in old wood - the creative power of the builder and the wear and tear of centuries of hard work.
The roseroot on the roof was planted as protection against lightning and fire. This too is part of History.

If only age could be strong, and youth wise.

MARTIN LUTHER

While the river Glomma breathes heavily in the December chill, Udnes Church has begun to put the Christmas decorations up.

What is life,
A breath in the reeds,
That dies down.
A play of forces
That yearn for
Eternity.

OEHLENSCHLÄGER

It is difficult not to believe in the cycle of rebirth when the world is slowly recreated on an August morning.
I wonder if St. Peter would book me in as a fjord-pony in a green meadow.

If you have a friend you trust, visit him often,
for the paths that are not walked are quickly overgrown.

ANONYMOUS

The buck seems to be powered by a coiled spring as he leaps over the floral water-colours of the lowland meadows.
The more sedate and easy-going sheep, on the other hand, prefer the uneven terrain of the Sirdal moorlands.
The very trees are so lazy here that they take a rest after the summer's hard work!

He risks less of a fall, who creeps along the ground
than he who climbs among the peaks.

SØREN KIERKEGAARD

The countdown to winter has begun at Ulnes in Vestre Slidre, but the cows are still enjoying the outdoor restaurant with its good views.

Young people want wide horizons,
old people want their home.

CORA SANDEL

Flowering potatoes under the high dome of the sky at Gran in Hadeland and undulating field and ravine landscape at Nannestad -
some of the attractions in the otherwise rather monotonous Eastern Norwegian farming districts.

Nature was in the director's chair when the farming land along Nordfjord was put together.
When the morning light wakes the landscape, frisky cows rise to their feet to start a new day in their green paradise.

We bind ourselves, even to the forces we tame.

STEIN MEHREN

The curving and winding ravine landscape of Enebakk, Akershus, became white and stiff when the sun yawned
and crawled into bed at winter solstice.

Where there is life, there is always something that grows,
and something that withers.

EIVIND BERGGRAV

The one day damp, drizzly and gunmetal-coloured just south of the capital,
the other crackling cold and red behind monumental oaks at Råde in Østfold.
In the inhabited country winter has many faces,
and which is the most beautiful depends on how you yourself feel.

Those who forget their parents are a stream without water,
a tree without roots.

CHINESE PROVERB

Why is the mining town of Røros so well-preserved? Because it spends much of the winter in the deep-freeze at minus 40°C!

It is better to light a candle than curse the darkness.

CONFUCIUS

Oslo is not only the seat of government, but the Holmenkollen ski-jump, the Vigeland Sculpture Park and the Royal Palace.
It is also a city of celebrations, which marks each New Year with vaulting ambitions and faith in itself as an important crossroads in the big wide world.

Where the light is strong, the shadow is deep.

GOETHE

© Natur og Kulturforlaget as 1994
Pb. 165, N-4441 Tonstad
Tel. +47 3837 0350
Fax: +47 3837 0670
Norway

PROJECT MANAGER: Snorre Aske
DESIGN: Cucumber
TYPESETTING: Cucumber
REPRODUCTION: Marthinsens Litho
PRINTING: Bryne Offset
COVER: Aske Trykkeri, Grafisk Effekt

First edition

This book is a love-letter to our beautiful
country and the scenery I love so much.
Together with all the best talents - from the
artistic to the select graphics producers - we
have created a unique book.
The quality of the picture reproductions
shows that a new high-water-mark has been
reached, thanks to state-of-the-art, raster-
less reproduction technology. The book also
has many other qualities that add up to a
new standard for such works. The team
behind Panorama Norway has done its very
best to give you, the reader, a real experience.

*I would like to thank everyone who has
made this publication possible:
In addition to his sharp eye, Pål Hermansen
has used a Fuji Panorama G 6x17 camera.
For bird and animal pictures he has used
35mm Nikon and Canon equipment.
Landscape and detail pictures were taken
with a Hasselblad (6x6cm) and a Arca large-
format camera (5x7").
The film is mainly Fujichrome Velvia.
Cucumber has edited the book and given it
an exciting design.
Marthinsen Litho have done pioneering
work with their new equipment for
raster-less Diamond Screening, supplied by
Pregraph A/S from Linotype Hell. They
used Kodak 2000 for this.
The choice of printing plates has also been
important for the quality. We have used
Horsell Capricorn II, positive offset plates
with Gemini conversion technology.
Bryne Offset has - as always - given us
outstanding print quality, as have Aske
Trykkeri / Grafisk Effekt, which have
printed and embossed the covers. The book
has been printed on Scheufelen's 170gm
Imperial Semi-Matt.
In conclusion I would like to thank
NOTRABOOKS for all its excellent support.*

Tonstad, September 1994

SNORRE ASKE

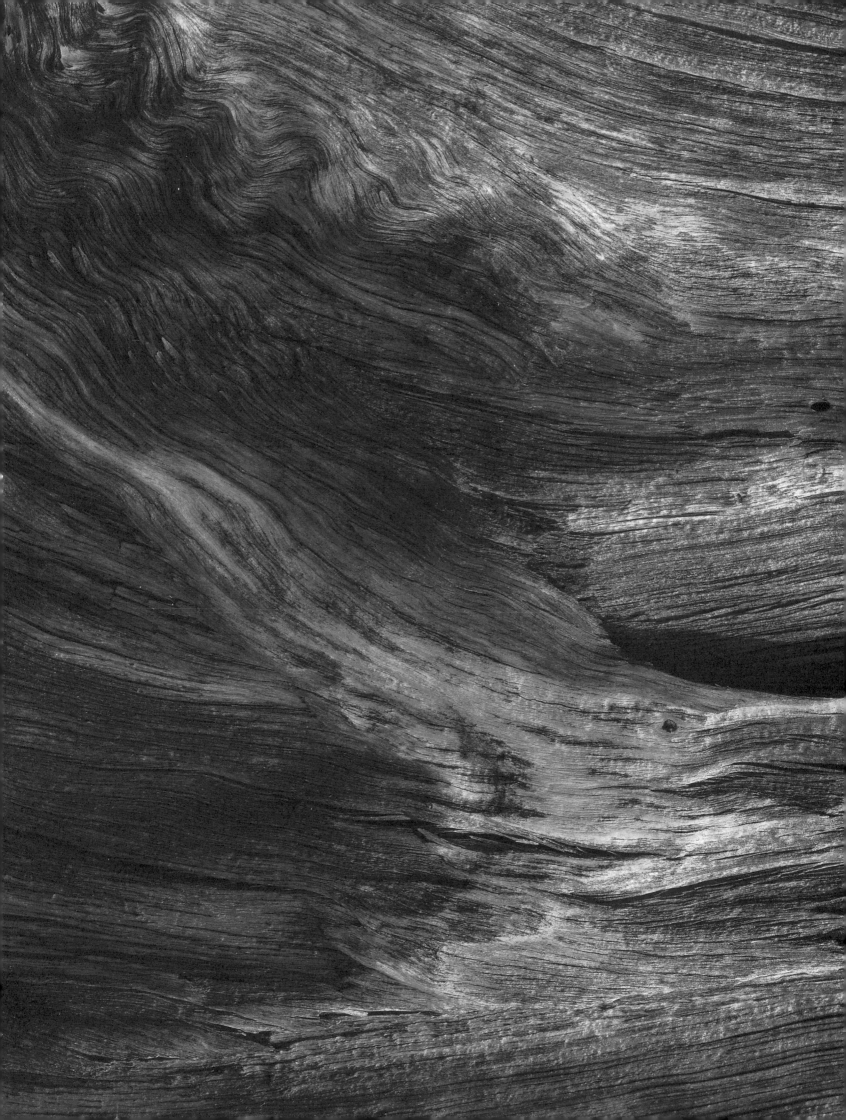

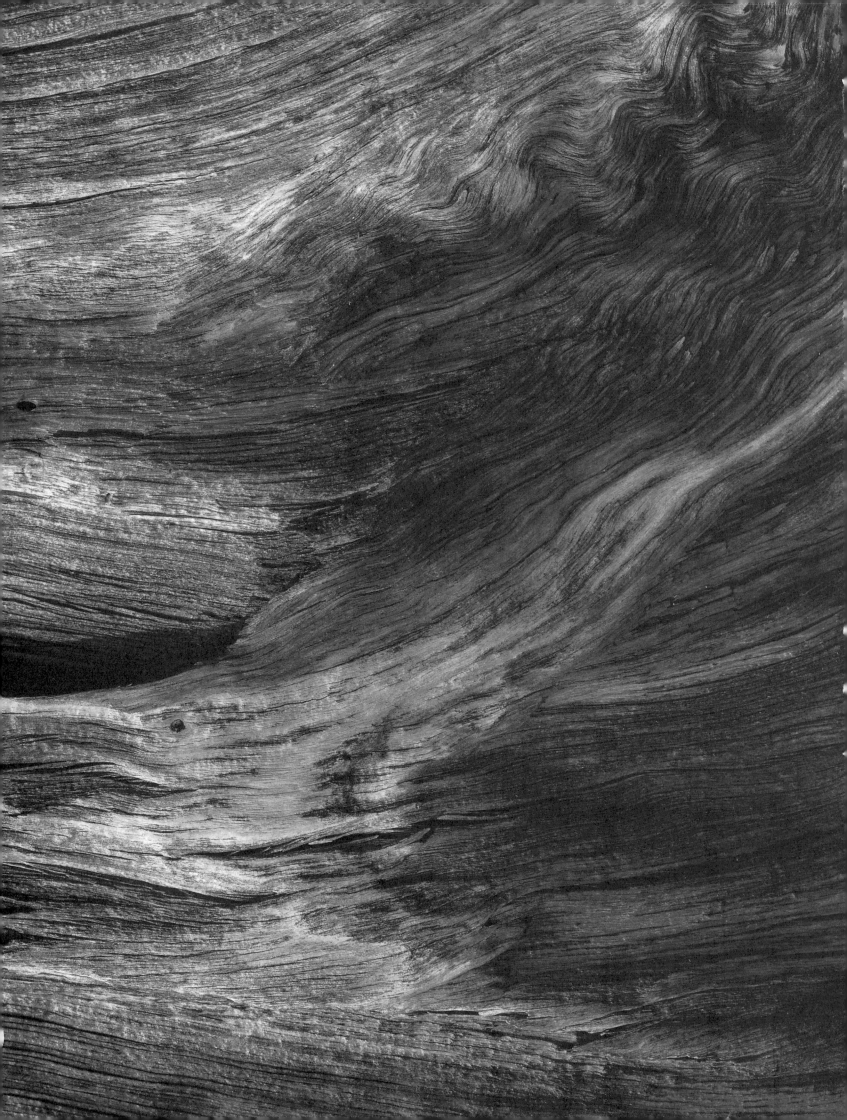